D0677027

PAINS
—*of*—
GLASS

TO ALL WHO FIND KING'S COLLEGE CHAPEL A PLACE OF
RENEWAL AND ENCOURAGEMENT

THE AUTHORS

GEORGE PATTISON has been Dean of Chapel at King's College, Cambridge, since
1991, having been a parish priest in Suffolk. In his scholarly work he focuses on
the philosophy of religion, and he is especially interested in Søren Kierkegaard,
the Danish thinker. He has also written and broadcast extensively on religion
and the arts, and his book *Art, Modernity and Faith*, has been described as 'full of
insights that artists, theorists and theologians should all find valuable'. He met
Sister Wendy Beckett some years ago, when looking at art books in a well-known
Cambridge bookshop.

SISTER WENDY BECKETT is a contemplative nun who lives in seclusion in the
grounds of a Carmelite monastery in Norfolk. She was educated at Oxford
University where she was awarded a Congratulatory First in English. A lifelong
art lover, Sister Wendy began to devote herself to the subject in 1980. She
writes regularly for art magazines as well as contributing to the arts pages of
national newspapers. Her previous books include *Art and the Sacred*
(Rider Books, 1992), and *Sister Wendy's Odyssey* (1993) and
Sister Wendy's Grand Tour (1994) for the BBC.

PAINS
—*of*—
GLASS

Sister Wendy Beckett
&
George Pattison

The Story of the Passion from
King's College Chapel, Cambridge

BBC BOOKS

ACKNOWLEDGEMENTS

I owe a considerable debt of gratitude to Hilary Wayment for extending and deepening my knowledge of the Chapel windows in the course of many conversations; also to James Whitbourn and David Kremer for their commitment to making *Pains of Glass* happen.

George Pattison

This book is published to accompany the television programme entitled *Pains of Glass* which was first broadcast in April 1995.

The programme was produced by James Whitbourn
Executive Producer David Kremer
Director Gary Boon

Published by BBC Books, an imprint of
BBC Worldwide Publishing,
BBC Worldwide Limited, Woodlands,
80 Wood Lane, London W12 OTT

First published 1995
© Sister Wendy Beckett and George Pattison, 1995
The moral right of the authors has been asserted
ISBN 0 563 37170 6

Edited by Gillian Forrester

Set in Caslon
Printed and bound in Great Britain by BPC Paulton Books Ltd, Paulton
Colour separations by Radstock Reproductions Ltd, Midsomer Norton
Jacket printed by Lawrence Allen Ltd, Weston-super-Mare
All photographs and College heraldry are reproduced by kind permission
of the Provost and Fellows of King's College,
Cambridge © reserved
BBC Books would like to thank George Pattison and the photographer
Mark Nicholson for their help with new photography.
Photograph of George Pattison © BBC

Cover and inside photographs of Sister Wendy Beckett © BBC,
photographer Justin Pumfrey

CONTENTS

THE WINDOWS

FOREWORDS

GEORGE PATTISON

Many people primarily associate King's College Chapel with the Festival of Nine Lessons and Carols, held on Christmas Eve and broadcast live world-wide. Perhaps the most poignant moment in that service comes at the very beginning when a solo treble voice sings the first verse of the carol, 'Once in Royal David's City'. From where I stand in the procession during the singing of this verse, I find myself looking at the great image of the Crucifixion in the East Window dominating the Chapel – a powerful reminder that the meaning of Christmas is inseparable from that of Holy Week and Easter. The stable points towards the cross, and to understand one, we have to understand the other. If the music of King's provides a unique treatment of Christmas, its stained glass windows offer a no less unique and no less powerful interpretation of the Passion.

As I shall explain in the Introduction, the Chapel windows were designed according to a scheme which linked New and Old Testament stories thematically. The Chapel windows contain a number of narratives, including scenes from the life of Christ and the Acts of the Apostles, but for this book we have chosen to focus specifically on the scenes of Christ's Passion, together with their Old Testament counterparts. The design of the book, showing Old and New Testament images on facing pages, reflects the scheme of pairings. Very occasionally we have chosen to omit certain Old Testament windows where the parallels are not strong, but we have included the majority of the scenes from the Passion narrative. The commentary takes the form of a dialogue between Sister Wendy Beckett and me, in which we progress window by window, exploring the iconographical scheme and reflecting on the religious significance of the images.

SISTER WENDY BECKETT

The stories in the Bible are not there for their narrative content: they are there primarily for their meaning. Christianity has always read all the Old Testament stories as prefiguring Christ, as ways of understanding his message, and who he was. In the same way, all the stories in the New Testament show not just what Jesus did, but what these deeds meant. So all the stories are luminous with divinity, translucent, and hence wonderfully suitable for the medium of stained glass. Light shines through the glass, making lovely abstract patterns, but it also lights up the pictures, revealing their beauty. There is a special beauty in these rare survivals of the way the Renaissance Church saw the Passion, because we too often see only the suffering. Here, in the King's College Chapel windows, we see the pain lit up with brightness, the Resurrection, as it were, shining through. It was a joy to look at them and try to share our reactions with you.

INTRODUCTION TO THE WINDOWS OF KING'S COLLEGE CHAPEL

King's College Chapel houses the greatest surviving scheme of pre-Reformation stained glass anywhere in Britain. It was installed between 1515 and 1531, a period which spanned the transition from the medieval to the Renaissance styles, and this important evolution is embodied in the design of the windows themselves. King's College was founded by Henry VI, but the work on the Chapel windows was begun during Henry VII's reign, and completed under Henry VIII. Since the Chapel was a royal commission, the best resources of the time were used. The overall iconographical scheme and choice of subjects for the windows were supervised by Richard Foxe, Bishop of Winchester, and, later, by John Fisher, Bishop of Rochester. Most of the designs featured in this book were drawn up by Dierick Vellert of Antwerp and executed by the King's Glazier Galyon Hone, who was also from the Low Countries. Hone was assisted by glaziers from the well-known 'Southwark School', such as Thomas Feve. The outstanding achievement of the glaziers is matched by the remarkable good fortune which enabled the windows to survive the Puritan revolution in the seventeenth century when many religious images were destroyed. William Dowsing, who spearheaded the assault on images in East Anglia, did survey the Chapel in 1643 for a fee of 6s 8d (the equivalent of 34 pence today!), noting the presence there of '1 thousand Supersticious Pictures', but happily no action was taken and the windows survived. Despite some accidental damage over the years, some restoration work and some new glass, what we see now is essentially what was originally envisaged.

The Chapel windows depict the narratives of the Life of the Virgin Mary, the Life, Passion and Resurrection of Christ and the Acts of the Apostles. Many are biblical stories, but their way of depicting the Bible may seem unusual today. The choice of subjects for the windows was based on an ancient system known as typology in which New Testament stories ('anti-types') are interpreted through Old Testament counterparts ('types'). Unlike prophecy, which entails making utterances or carrying out deliberate prophetic actions which predict the future, typology draws on events or actions which were prophetic in ways unknown to those involved in them. In the New Testament, for instance, the crossing of the Red Sea by the Israelites is seen as a 'type' of the redemption of humanity by Christ. The Gospel of St Matthew records that Jesus himself compared his burial and resurrection with Jonah's ordeal in the belly of the whale (see p. 43).

This method of linking Old and New Testaments became widespread in the Middle Ages, popularized through books such as the *Biblia Pauperum* which provided the basis for some of the King's College Chapel designs. The contracts for the windows of 1526 specify that they should portray 'the olde lawe and the new lawe', and the scenes were therefore arranged in pairs which were to be read vertically so that the lower range of images shows the narrative of the life of Christ, whilst the upper range shows a series of Old Testament and Apocryphal scenes which function as types of the pictures below. Many of these links might be regarded by modern biblical scholars as arbitrary and absurd – yet, as we hope to show here, even the most curious uses of typology can help to rescue the stories they tell from over-familiarity, inviting us to see them afresh, as if for the first time. There is one major exception to this arrangement in the windows we discuss in this book, and that is the scheme of the great East Window which in a series of six images shows the condemnation and crucifixion of Jesus without any accompanying types; this arrangement suggests that this event was too great and its meaning too plain to need any commentary.

George Pattison

PLAN OF THE WINDOWS OF THE CHAPEL

The whole Chapel is given in outline, and the detail shows Windows 8–17 which illustrate the scenes of Christ's Passion and their Old Testament and Apocryphal counterparts. These windows are listed below with those not discussed or illustrated in the book italicized.

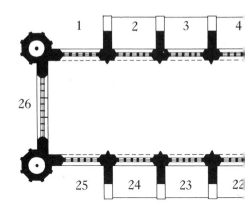

8.1	*Elisha Raises the Shunammite's Son*	13.2	Pilate Washing his Hands
		13.3	Christ Carrying the Cross
8.2	*The Raising of Lazarus*	13.4	Christ Nailed to the Cross
8.3	The Triumph of David	13.5	The Crucifixion
8.4	Christ's Entry into Jerusalem	13.6	The Descent from the Cross
9.1	The Israelites Gathering Manna	*14.1*	*The Brazen Serpent*
		14.2	*Naomi and her Daughters-in-law Mourning*
9.2	The Last Supper		
9.3	The Fall of the Rebel Angels	14.3	The Lamentation of Christ
9.4	The Agony in the Garden	15.1	Joseph Cast into the Pit
10.1	Cain and Abel	15.2	The Entombment of Christ
10.2	The Betrayal of Christ	*15.3*	*The Exodus*
10.3	*Shimei Cursing David*	*15.4*	*The Harrowing of Hell*
10.4	The Mocking of Christ	16.1	Jonah Cast up by the Whale
11.1	Jeremiah Imprisoned	16.2	The Resurrection of Christ
11.2	Christ before Annas	*16.3*	*Tobias's Return to his Mother*
11.3	The Shame of Noah	*16.4*	*Christ's Appearance to the Virgin*
11.4	Christ before Herod		
12.1	Job Tormented	17.1	Reuben at the Empty Pit
12.2	The Scourging of Christ	17.2	The Three Marys at the Tomb
12.3	Solomon Crowned by Bathsheba	*17.3*	*Daniel in the Lions' Den*
12.4	The Crowning with Thorns	17.4	Christ Appears to Mary Magdalene
13.1	Christ Shown to the People		

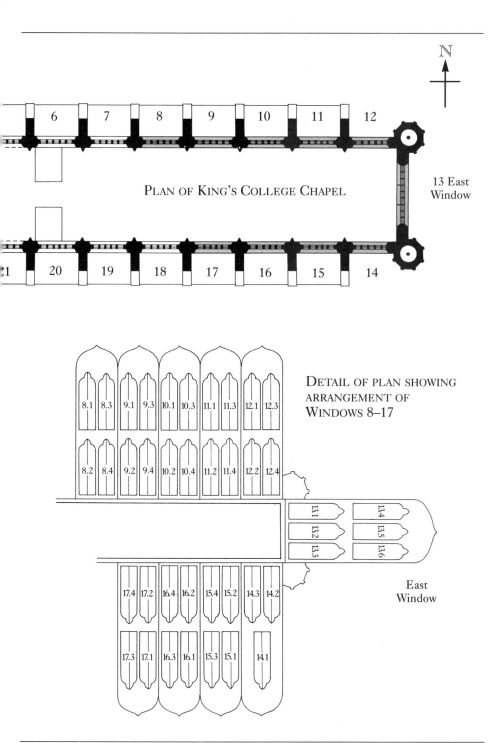

N

6 7 8 9 10 11 12

PLAN OF KING'S COLLEGE CHAPEL

13 East
Window

21 20 19 18 17 16 15 14

DETAIL OF PLAN SHOWING
ARRANGEMENT OF
WINDOWS 8–17

| 8.1 | 8.3 | 9.1 | 9.3 | 10.1 | 10.3 | 11.1 | 11.3 | 12.1 | 12.3 |
| 8.2 | 8.4 | 9.2 | 9.4 | 10.2 | 10.4 | 11.2 | 11.4 | 12.2 | 12.4 |

13.1 13.4
13.2 13.5
13.3 13.6

East
Window

17.4 17.2 16.4 16.2 15.4 15.2 14.3 14.2

17.3 17.1 16.3 16.1 15.3 15.1 14.1

CHRIST'S ENTRY INTO JERUSALEM

- *Matthew 21: 1-11*
- *Mark 11: 1-10*
- *Luke 19: 1-9, 29-38*
- *John 12: 12-15*

GP The first scene of the Passion series shows Jesus's triumphant entry into Jerusalem, the first Palm Sunday. In this window two different gospel stories seem to have been conflated since above Jesus, in a tree, is a figure who is almost certainly Zacchaeus, whom Jesus met in Jericho before he arrived at Jerusalem. Zacchaeus is relevant to the theme of Palm Sunday, however, because he is someone who could change. A rich tax collector, who used extortion to make his living, he none the less threw aside his pride and clambered up a tree to catch sight of Jesus. The punch-line of that story, 'Today salvation has come to this house', is a wonderful motto for Palm Sunday itself, since salvation is coming to Jerusalem, even though those watching are not aware of it.

WB Yes, they're not looking in the right place, and their response is conveyed pictorially by making Jerusalem such a stony city, with that massive, dead architecture. Yet, in contrast, there is the living tree with Zacchaeus, the man who did repent, sitting in it. I'm sorry that Jesus can't see him because Zacchaeus might have brought a smile to his sad face. Jesus recognizes that not many people are going to listen to what he's come to tell them; he knows these people are not really welcoming the kingdom of Heaven into their lives, despite their great excitement.

WINDOW 8.4; DETAIL

THE TRIUMPH OF DAVID

• *1 Samuel 18: 6-7*

GP This scene prefigures the Passion story of Christ's entry into Jerusalem. David is returning in triumph to Jerusalem after his successful battle with the Philistines. He carries the head of the giant Goliath on a sword and is being greeted by the people of the city, who are cheering and playing musical instruments, a scene of merriment and jollity. There is a close link between David and Jesus, since Jesus was regarded as the prophesied heir of the house of David. They also represent two different value systems, however, as David was a man of blood whose idea of monarchy was to do with worldly power, and more Mafia boss than saint.

WB David is a young man at the beginning of what he sees as a career of great glory, but he doesn't realize that it will also bring much pain, suffering and spiritual failure. He has no idea of what it really means to be a true king. He's dressed to the nines and proudly bearing aloft the sign of his triumph, whereas Jesus, dressed in a simple robe, virtually without decoration, does know what it means to be a spiritual king and can only feel sadness. In the Bible David was a frail youth who killed a giant, but the artists have made him a rather hefty, glamorous, young man. This emphasizes the contrast with Jesus, who is not an heroic prince, but a humble man riding sadly on a donkey.

WINDOW 8.3

THE LAST SUPPER

- *Matthew 26: 17-29*
- *Mark 14: 12-25*
- *Luke 22: 7 -23*
- *John 13: 21-30*

GP The narrative sequence of the windows goes straight from Palm Sunday to the Last Supper, shown here as the Jewish feast of the Passover, which celebrated the escape of the Israelites from Egypt. If you look closely, you can see there's a piece of roasted lamb on the big dish in the middle of the table. The centre-piece of the action is Jesus giving the morsel of bread to Judas, who will betray him; an intimate bonding between the saviour and his betrayer. Below, on the right, we can see a jug and bowl, which remind us about another part of the story, when Jesus washed the disciples' feet.

WB I'm glad that you've identified which one Judas is in the picture because the Apostles on the whole look a rather villainous lot, and quite a few of them could have been Judas. Peter and John are on either side of Jesus looking anxious, and the rest of the Apostles are just not very interested in the important actions taking place in their midst. It's so comforting to see them, unaware of what's going on, because we sometimes feel that Jesus was surrounded only by holy people. Actually, they were just like us, like that Apostle in the middle above Judas who looks as though he's arguing across the table.

WINDOW 9.2

THE ISRAELITES GATHERING MANNA

- *Exodus 16: 11-36*
- *Numbers 11: 7-9*

GP After their flight from Egypt, the Israelites wandered in the wilderness and feared starvation, but God promised to provide, and showered them with manna. Up in the top left corner you can see God sitting in the heavens, smiling benignly down on His people, in contrast to how, at the Last Supper, Jesus is in the middle of the action. The link between these two windows is one which shouldn't surprise us, as the theme of the feeding of the Israelites with manna is in Christian hymns and prayers closely connected with the Last Supper or Eucharist, where Jesus gives himself in the form of the bread.

WB The glorious brightness and abundance of this window contrast poignantly with the relative austerity and lack of harmony in the scene of the Last Supper, where Jesus is giving something that costs everything, his own body and blood. It doesn't really cost God to give the manna – it's just a mark of his love. The Israelites seem to have such security compared to the anxious Apostles, and Moses is standing with great serenity, holding the stone tablets of the Law, the written commandments. Moses prefigures Jesus at the Last Supper giving a new commandment, 'Love one another, as I have loved you'. The Ten Commandments can be taken simply as rules of conduct, but Jesus's new commandment goes right to the heart.

WINDOW 9.1; DETAIL

THE AGONY IN THE GARDEN

- *Matthew 26: 36-46*
- *Mark 14: 32-42*

GP Christ is in the Garden of Gethsemane after the Last Supper and immediately before his arrest. He is praying to his Father, asking that the cup of suffering might pass from him, but none the less submitting himself to the Father's will. The picture is dominated by the lone figure of Christ. His physical posture is one of total trust and openness. He's not praying as people often pray in church, hands together and heads bowed; instead, he's looking up, hands open, totally vulnerable and receptive to the will of God. Perhaps this is the most human image of Jesus, and yet, in a sense, it's a more decisive moment than the Crucifixion. For until this point he could have turned back, but from here on he's completely given over to the Father's will.

WB I find this, of all the windows, the one that moves me most, because it is such a wonderful visual image of Jesus's isolation. It's one of the instances where the stone bar dividing the window fits so superbly into the meaning of the picture. Jesus is absolutely cut off from human support, because the Apostles are sleeping at the bottom of the picture, and from divine support, because he can't see the angel from where he is. It's as if he prays into a nothingness, and yet he has complete confidence that he will be held by his father. That picture of Jesus in his weakness is more encouraging to us than practically any other image in the scriptures.

WINDOW 9.4

THE FALL OF THE REBEL ANGELS

- *Luke 10: 18*
- *Revelation 12: 7-9*

GP If the Agony in the Garden is a picture of humility, of submission to God's will, this window, by contrast, shows the manifestation of pride and rebellion. The angel Lucifer (Satan) and his hosts, who rebelled against God, are being cast out of Heaven by the Archangel Michael and his angels. It's a very dramatic window, an almost expressionistic blaze of colour and confusion of forms. As the battle rages the Rebel Angels lose their angelic shapes, and are turned into horrible monstrosities heaped on top of each other, and thrown in a great jumble out of heaven. The rebel angels represent chaos, and are shown in these animal-like, demon-like forms because they have lost personality, the highest good.

WB It's very difficult to read this window, and the great chaos at the bottom which shows the consequences of opposing God contrasts visually with the lucidity and clear lines of the Agony in the Garden which is concerned with the desire to do God's will. What also strikes me is the contrast between God, sitting there at the top looking sadly on and removed from us, and Jesus, who lives in our world. That's the image of Jesus which keeps us going, whereas that other image of God seems too remote. I am also touched here by the theme of obedience and disobedience, because to me the greatest strength of Jesus was his obedience.

WINDOW 9.3; DETAIL

17

THE BETRAYAL OF CHRIST

- *Matthew 26: 47-56*
- *Mark 14: 43-52*
- *Luke 22: 47-53*
- *John 18: 1-12*

GP The Garden of Gethsemane is now completely transformed by the great crowd of soldiers and servants of the High Priest carrying spears and torches, who have come to arrest Jesus. Their faces are depersonalized by helmets and visors, so they are more like dreadful machines than human beings. Judas kisses Jesus, a pre-arranged sign to the soldiers that this is the man they are to arrest, and while Jesus is being betrayed, his closest friend Peter is showing that he still hasn't understood Jesus's message of non-violence because he is cutting off the High Priest's servant's ear with his sword.

WB Fortunately we know what happens next, that Jesus will stretch across and heal the ear, but the picture has caught wonderfully the sense of violence being suddenly unleashed. The tragic thing is that Peter thinks he's being a friend, whereas he is betraying Jesus just as much as Judas is. All the other Apostles seem to have run away. How much movement and violence and excitement there is in this picture! And there is just one oasis of calm, the face of Jesus, so resolute, almost impassively accepting the kiss of Judas. He lets Judas clasp him, and he clasps Judas back, and, as we know, says to him, 'Friend, do what you are here to do'. That refusal to let his inner agony show on his face makes this image very poignant for me.

CAIN AND ABEL

• *Genesis 4: 1-15*

GP This window shows Cain killing his brother Abel, the very first murder recorded in the Bible. A comparison between these two windows suggests to me that the betrayal of Jesus was like a betrayal of a brother by a brother, and the Crucifixion therefore an act of fratricide. At an earlier stage of the story the brothers made offerings to God. Cain brought crops he had harvested, and Abel sacrificed the best of his flock. Abel's offering was accepted by God, but Cain's was rejected. A lot of modern readers feel that Cain was treated unjustly, but the crux of the story is that Cain didn't love God or his brother, so the murder was not just a response to God's rejection of his offering, but the outward manifestation of the envy and rivalry already in Cain's heart.

WB I think the whole point of the story is that Cain hadn't done his best, and was just going through the motions, whereas Abel gave to God something which really mattered to him. We can never tell what is in someone else's heart, however. It might seem to us that people give or don't give, and we are often utterly mistaken. Only God knows what you intend, and the real lesson there is that God sees through the trappings and knows what is in the human heart, whatever people do. Abel has something of that look of resigned acceptance which is in Jesus's face in the scene of the betrayal.

WINDOW 10.1; DETAIL

THE MOCKING OF CHRIST

• *Matthew 26: 67*
• *Mark 14: 65*
• *Luke 22: 63*

GP Jesus is in the house of Annas, the father-in-law of Caiaphas, the High Priest. Jesus has been blindfolded and is being struck by his captors, who are shouting 'Now, Messiah, if you are a prophet, tell us who hit you'. The artist has really gone to town in depicting the brutality and coarseness of the scene, and has given Jesus's tormentors rough peasant faces full of hatred and venom. The scribes and elders are looking on (see detail, right), and may think themselves above the mob, but they are conniving in what is happening by their failure to act. One of the terrible things about this picture is that those people are the ones with the power, but are cowardly, and don't want to step out of line.

WB This is the kind of picture I find painful to look at, because it's bad enough to suffer, but to be mocked when you are suffering seems inhuman. The artist has carefully put Jesus on a raised platform, as if he is in a theatre for people to laugh at him. Jesus is showing a sweet dignity, with his large hands folded patiently, while others make fools of themselves. What I find particularly painful is that the dog, an innocent creature, has been brought in to share in the complicity of human nastiness. Those in authority are safe in their alcoves, looking on and doing nothing, and I'm especially upset by the way the man on the right, probably Annas, is leaning on a cushion, making himself comfortable while he watches someone suffering.

WINDOW 10.4; DETAILS

CHRIST BEFORE ANNAS

• *John 18: 12-23*

GP This window shows Jesus actually before Annas, surrounded by soldiers and being questioned about his teaching. The wording on Annas' throne, *sic respondes pontifice*, or 'Is that the way to answer the High Priest?', refers to the rebuke given to Jesus by one of the soldiers, according to St John's Gospel. Jesus replied by saying, 'If I was wrong to speak what I did, produce evidence to prove it; if I was right, why strike me?'. The motif of mockery which dominated the earlier scene is repeated in this picture, and the men are pulling what I suppose they think are funny faces. There is also real violence here, however, and the artist has taken pains to show us the instruments of violence – the clubs with spikes and the spears they are carrying, as well as the armour of the figure in front.

WB The foreground of the picture is dominated by that man's great sword jutting up at an angle, and his purple boots which look so forceful. The architecture is also very powerful, and so overwhelming that it can't even be contained by the picture: the top of the building and the great blue canopy hanging over the High Priest seem to jut out into space. Jesus stands there, just accepting the taunts and the brutality, with that enormous chain around his neck which they've forced him to wear as if he would escape if they left him for a moment.

WINDOW 11.2; DETAIL

JEREMIAH IMPRISONED

• *Jeremiah 32*

GP This window shows one of the most Christ-like of the Old Testament prophets, Jeremiah, being taken away to prison. Jeremiah's story relates to the New Testament scene, because, like Jesus, he not only prophesied that a new Law would come, but also lived according to it. Jeremiah also taught that the spiritual salvation of the Hebrews would come about only through the experience of oppression and suffering, but when he warned the people of Jerusalem that they couldn't sustain their independence against the various powers oppressing them, they didn't want to hear the truth and locked him away.

WB Jeremiah is a wonderful example of somebody who doesn't mind what the politics of a situation are, but simply looks at what his heart tells him. The time came when his oppressors had to recognize that what Jeremiah said was absolutely true. As with the picture of Christ before Annas, the great crushing architecture seems to represent the massive authority of the state. Any security which depends on externals, upon architecture and power, must be false, however. True security can only exist in the heart, and this is why Jesus can stand in chains being spat at and jostled, and yet have a face which, though sad, is utterly secure.

WINDOW 11.1; DETAIL

CHRIST BEFORE HEROD

• *Luke 23: 8-12*

GP Jesus has been dragged through the great triumphal arch by a posse of soldiers with pikes and staffs, and is now standing before Herod, ruler of Galilee and symbol of secular authority. There is extraordinary assurance in the figure of Herod, who had hoped to see something interesting, a miracle worker, but is instead looking at this pathetic specimen in chains with bare feet who refuses to reply to his questioning. The man on the extreme left points at Jesus, a jabbing, accusatory gesture which shows inhuman contempt for a fellow human being. On the arch above the allegorical figure with a club in its hand is possibly Hercules, a symbol of male worldly power, whereas Jesus's way is something rather different.

WB When you think of the other incidents which could have been shown, such as Peter denying Christ, for example, the choice of this subject, and the previous scene of Christ before Annas is obviously significant. It is as if the artists really wanted to emphasize power and the strength of weakness. Both pictures are saying much the same, though one shows religious and the other secular authority: both show weighty, extravagant architecture, and somebody enthroned in power. Jesus does not even challenge Herod with a look. He holds his peace, keeping to the choice he has made to let his Father have his way.

WINDOW 11.4; DETAIL

24

THE SHAME OF NOAH

• *Genesis 9: 20-27*

GP This is one of the most extraordinary images of all the chapel windows. To our modern way of thinking, the choice of a drunken old man to illustrate the suffering of Christ might seem odd and startling, but the point is that Noah's nakedness is exposed, something that was shocking in his culture. Although his son Shem is trying to cover him up, his other sons Ham and Japheth are mocking him, and his exposure and humiliation is the key link between this picture and the scene of Christ before Herod. Ham is holding a vine, and this alludes both to Noah's role as the founder of viticulture and to the motif of Israel as a vine planted and tended by God. Here there is the particular association of wine with the cup of suffering, which through the sacrament of communion is also a symbol for us of being called to share in Christ's sufferings.

WB Jesus says that the wine has been drawn from his own person, and is his own blood, so it's a very profound image at many levels. Noah in his drunkenness looks dead, so the picture might also be read as a prefiguring of Jesus drinking the cup and passing into death. There is also another curious analogy in that when people are drunk they lose their normal sense of self, and in the Passion Jesus himself abandons self. But since he has always given himself, he has nothing to fear, as it were, in entering into the drunkenness of the Passion.

WINDOW 11.3; DETAIL

THE SCOURGING OF CHRIST

- *Mark 15: 15*
- *Luke 23: 16 and 22*

GP Jesus has been handed over to the Roman soldiers by Pontius Pilate, the governor of Judaea, to be flogged before being crucified. He is tied to a red column, exposed and vulnerable, and is being beaten by a thuggish-looking soldier while others press in with birches and whips. Some of the earlier scenes showed psychological or spiritual torture, but this is an image of straightforward physical cruelty. For the first time in this narrative, however, one person is prepared to speak up for Jesus: Pilate's wife, who had dreamed of Jesus, is shown above on the left, looking towards her husband with a mournful, beseeching face, but he's turning away from her.

WB I also find this picture, terrible as it is, less terrible than those in which Jesus is being mocked. Despite that look of brutish harshness, the scourger is treating Christ as another human being, rather than mocking him as someone beneath human dignity. The faces are our faces, rather crude, but not those almost inhuman faces of the mockers. Jesus is looking away towards the Father and praying, a perfect example of what we should do when people are being unkind to us. What I particularly like about Pilate's wife is that she isn't urging Pilate to act with justice and love towards Jesus out of religious motives, but because she knows it's wrong to treat an innocent man like that; it's just an act of human goodness.

WINDOW 12.2

JOB TORMENTED

• *Job 2: 7-9*

GP In this picture we see Job's wife, a very different kind of woman from Pilate's wife – one who isn't taking the part of the sufferer. Job, the epitome of righteous suffering, has refused to abandon God in the face of misfortune. Some very ugly-looking devils are raining down blows on him, and his wife is spurning him and encouraging him to 'Curse God, and die!'. She is portrayed as a very imperious figure, looking down on him with contempt. We speak of the patience of Job, but he continually rails against God, and is shown here as a man who is on the verge of defeat, whereas the depiction of Christ being scourged is an image of someone victorious in suffering.

WB This is a wonderful image of the reality that we all have to live and suffer and die alone. There is no indication in the Book of Job that it wasn't a happy enough marriage, but the fact that when he's reduced to extremity she isn't with him is a poetic expression of the truth that no one can go into the abyss with you, except God. In the same way, Jesus, although he has a sympathizer, still suffers alone. Unlike Job, who seems rather self-pitying, Jesus isn't concerned at all with the details of his suffering, and looks out with confidence to his Father, trusting that all will be redeemed. It's a contrast between suffering used to good purpose, and suffering endured, which are two quite different things.

WINDOW 12.1

27

THE CROWNING WITH THORNS

• *Matthew 27: 27-31*
• *Mark 15: 16-20*

GP This is another scene of mocking, which contains both psychological and physical torture. The soldiers have led Jesus into the courtyard of Pilate's house, dressed him in a purple robe and placed the crown of thorns on his head . They are mockingly calling out 'Hail, King of the Jews!', as they laugh and jeer at him. One thing in this picture which always strikes me is the face of the man behind Jesus; it has faded with the passage of time, but this has had the dramatic effect of dehumanizing his face so that it is almost like an impersonal, impassive mask. This is perhaps the only point in the sequence so far when we see Jesus looking almost defeated. This window shows real suffering, not something which just comes and goes, but which comes again and again.

WB I find this a particularly affecting image because, as you say, it's the one time when you can see the cumulative effects of what Jesus has suffered. It's almost as if the windows we have seen represent a series of hammer-blows, one instance of suffering after another, and now Jesus can't even summon up the energy to hold the sceptre he has been given. He can only clench his hands and keep going. His feet, too, are twisted with the pain of someone who's using every single ounce of energy just to stay upright and not collapse.

WINDOW 12.4; DETAIL

SOLOMON CROWNED BY BATHSHEBA

• *1 Kings*

GP The mocking of Christ illustrates the Christian perception of true kingship – the strength that is made perfect in weakness. This window also shows us sovereignty, though it is a different kind of image of kingship. Bathsheba, who is David's wife and Solomon's mother, is crowning Solomon as king. It's a gorgeous scene; Bathsheba, who is very beautiful, is wearing a wonderful tasselled dress, and Solomon is young and good-looking, with long blonde hair, and sits on a splendid throne. Incidentally, Solomon looks remarkably like Henry VII, a benefactor of King's College, and I think that this likeness may be intentional. There seems to be a world of difference between the young, handsome, wise monarch assuming his splendid earthly throne, and Christ, an almost defeated man, crowned with thorns, mocked and laughed at – they seem like inverted mirror-images of each other.

WB I also notice in this window the lovely green meadows and the water stretching beyond the city, as if to suggest that Solomon has the whole world there to enjoy. Jesus, by contrast, seems compressed, and that blue pillar above looks as if it might crush him. One of the things that suffering does to you is to confine you, so you can't get out of it. The Passion story tells us that although Jesus was imprisoned, and without human hope, he still could redeem us. He is the man from whom we draw our strength, not the handsome king.

WINDOW 12.3; DETAIL

29

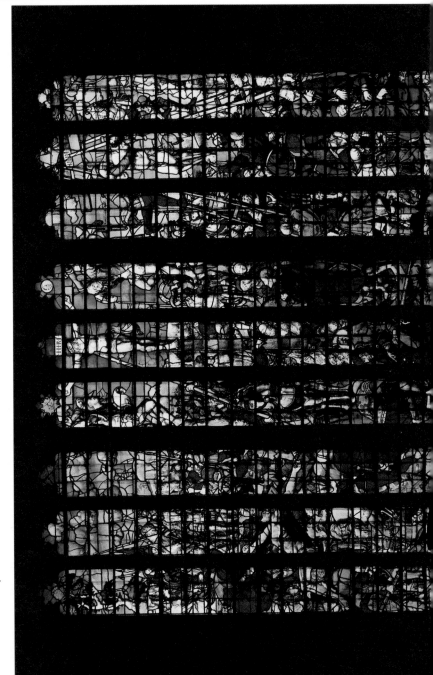

THE EAST WINDOW

Top row (left to right): Christ Nailed to the Cross; The Crucifixion; The Descent from the Cross

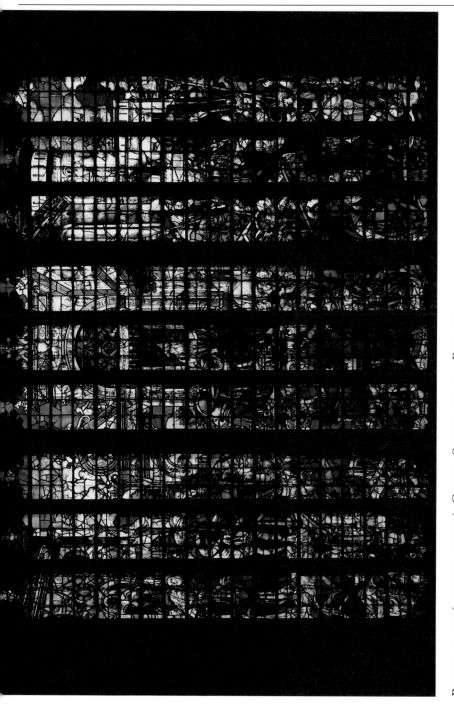

BOTTOM ROW (LEFT TO RIGHT): CHRIST SHOWN TO THE PEOPLE;
PILATE WASHING HIS HANDS; CHRIST CARRYING THE CROSS

CHRIST SHOWN TO THE PEOPLE (ECCE HOMO)

• *John 19: 4-6*

GP Pilate, the figure on the left, has brought Jesus onto the balcony to show him to the crowd. Pilate says 'Behold the man (*Ecce homo*); I am bringing him out to let you know that I find no case against him', but the chief priests and crowd shout 'Crucify! Crucify!'. Christ stands there, less a king or God than a human being, a creature of flesh and blood who has been flogged, tortured and tormented. I think it's very striking that one of the figures shouting up at him is wearing what looks like a bishop's mitre. Scenes of the Last Judgement from the Middle Ages very often include a few bishops, kings, monks, nuns and friars among the wicked, as if to remind us that participating in the externals of the Church isn't enough to put us on the right side.

WB It's interesting to contrast the bitter and taunting face of the mitred priest with Pilate's noble, sorrowing face diagonally opposite. Pilate is really unhappy about what is happening, and is still trying to save Jesus. Yet, as you say, externals do not make a holy person, and the distress Pilate is clearly experiencing doesn't affect the fact that he has brought Jesus out to be condemned, and that he will soon move to the judgement seat to consolidate his decision. It comes down to choices; we all have to choose what we want, and Pilate ultimately wants his own political stability rather than justice.

WINDOW 13.1

PILATE WASHING HIS HANDS

• *Matthew 27: 24-25*

GP Here Pilate is enthroned in the judgement seat with all the pomp and circumstance of a monarch, and Jesus is below him, his hair pulled back by the heavily-armoured soldier wearing a visor. Pilate is holding his hands over a bowl as his servant pours water over them, and saying, 'My hands are clean of this man's blood'. The figure is vividly portrayed as the eager servant helping his master. He is doing his duty, like the other servants below, who are dragging Christ away to be crucified. Pilate's abdication of responsibility is one of the most common human reactions to being involved in evil.

WB Pilate's gesture is ironic, because he is there in all the splendour of authority, with space and dignity and grandeur, and yet is pretending that nothing that is happening is to do with him. It is wonderfully symbolic that Jesus is shown from behind: we have the full face of worldly power in the figure of Pilate, but Jesus is depicted as a bent figure, his face twisted by somebody else to reveal that suffering profile. This back view of Jesus suggests that he is entering deep into the darkness. It's the world that is in the light, and the spirit that is shown from behind, and bowed.

WINDOW 13.2

CHRIST CARRYING THE CROSS

• *John 19: 17*

GP   This window shows the Way of the Cross. Jesus is staggering under the heavy cross, dragged along on a rope by the ugly and brutish-looking soldier on the right, who has the sort of grotesque face which late medieval artists loved to portray. But there is also another kind of face, that of Veronica looking up at Jesus in sorrow and pity, and holding up her handkerchief to him to wipe away the blood and sweat and dust. His divine compassion meets her human compassion; they are joined together by this act of mutual love, and isolated in the middle of the mob.

WB   I think that Jesus and Veronica are the most purely beautiful images that we have seen. His face and hers are so infinitely sorrowful, but both are sorrowing not for themselves, but for the other. Jesus is imprisoned by the angle of the cross, but unaware of it, because he's giving all his compassion to this grieving woman, and she is oblivious of how her action will appear to others, because she is giving to this suffering man. I find this a confusing picture because there is so much in it – there is the great weight of power above Christ and Veronica, and all I really want to see are just those two faces, faces of people in great pain but expressing selfless love, so that it might become a beautiful picture instead of a horrific one.

CHRIST NAILED TO THE CROSS

GP This window shows the horrific scene of Christ being nailed to the cross. We are so used to seeing crucifixes – in churches, in religious shops, in homes and around people's necks – that it's easy to forget what they are actually depicting. This picture shows us the stark reality of what crucifixion actually means, a man being nailed to a cross and tortured to death in a peculiarly horrible and painful manner. The workmen are going about their task of hammering the nails in a very efficient manner, treating it as a job to be done, and they don't show a flicker of hesitation or compassion.

WB I am very struck by how the effort of the executioners is matched and balanced by the energy shown by Jesus in receiving the pain. His body is not passively yielding; there's a holy tension, as if he's holding himself clenched to embrace the cross. The whole picture is alive with energy, some of it misdirected, some of it superbly directed, but there is no hiding-place there, as it were. You are either hammering the nails in or, like Jesus, you are accepting the nails actively, because that is the way of redemption. Jesus is completely surrounded, yet he is completely alone.

WINDOW 13.4

THE CRUCIFIXION

- *Matthew 27: 33-56*
- *Mark 15: 22-41*
- *Luke 23: 33 -49*
- *John 19: 17-37*

GP This window shows the Crucifixion, the central image of the Passion story. At this point Mary, the mother of Jesus, is brought into the narrative, and is shown looking at the Apostle John. Before his death Jesus had told them to care for each other, saying 'Mother, here is your son', and 'Son, here is your mother'. John is always depicted as a very young man, someone who needs the nurturing that Mary is turning to give him. She's forgetting about her own suffering in caring for his.

WB The image of the soldiers dicing for Jesus's garments under the cross is painfully explicit. There is a strong contrast between those who are seeking God, and those who are quite unaware of what is happening. The fact that the centurion on the left is piercing Jesus's side with a spear means that Jesus has actually died. I used to feel great grief during Holy Week, and I still sometimes do. One Holy Week it suddenly struck me that it must have been a tremendous moment of joy for Jesus to be able to say to his Father that he had done all he had been asked to do. It must have been a death of unimaginable joy, but everybody else in the picture is either grieving or doesn't understand at all.

WINDOW 13.5

THE DESCENT FROM THE CROSS

- *Matthew 27: 57-58*
- *Mark 15: 42-46*
- *Luke 23: 50-54*
- *John 19: 38-40*

GP Joseph of Arimathaea, a man of means who was a secret disciple of Jesus, has obtained permission from Pilate to bury Jesus's body. He stands on the left-hand ladder and Nicodemus, a Pharisee who visited Jesus at night for teaching, reaches up in the centre to grasp the nail which still pierces Jesus's feet. This picture shows us a very human pain, doesn't it? Mary, having cared for John, has now collapsed, as many mothers would on the death of their sons, and it is John's turn, with the help of Mary Magdalene, to care for her.

WB Up until now Jesus has been the main actor, but now he is with the Father, and only his body remains, so the whole emphasis of the story has changed. For those involved it's seemingly become worse, because now that Jesus is dead they have nothing left, just practical steps to take and great grief to endure. We can understand Mary's heartbroken collapse, but for us who know the outcome, the pain has gone already. While Jesus is still being taken down from the cross, we are seeing the light of the Resurrection. We can feel the most enormous gratitude for what has been done for us, and we just have to put out our hands and receive it.

WINDOW 13.6

THE LAMENTATION OF CHRIST

GP Jesus has been taken down from the cross, and his body is surrounded by those who loved him most. Here we see him cradled once more in his mother's arms as he was when a baby. Joseph of Arimathaea is at Jesus's head, and Mary Magdalene stands besides him, with another of the woman, Nicodemus, and perhaps John. Grouped around Jesus, they perform the very last tasks they can do for him as a human being in order to prepare his body for burial. In an extraordinarily vivid touch the artist has shown the bowl with a sponge half-covered in blood that has been used for washing away the marks of suffering from the body, and, on the ground, the pincers and the nails.

WB What I find so moving here is that we know, and nobody in the picture knows, that this is not the end for Jesus. One grieves with them, a total grief, but underneath is our secret knowledge that soon their grief is to be turned into the most overwhelming joy.

THE ENTOMBMENT OF CHRIST

- *Matthew 27: 57-61*
- *Mark 15: 42-47*
- *Luke 23: 50-55*
- *John 19: 38-42*

GP Here we see Joseph of Arimathaea at Jesus's head and Nicodemus holding the feet, lowering the body with great tenderness and love into the tomb. The Apostle John, Jesus's mother Mary, and one of the Marys are grouped behind, and Mary Magdalene kneels before the body, the crown of thorns beside her. This is the last act of love and care that they can carry out for Jesus, and there is something very powerful about that tenderness and way of loving. I remember once hearing an undertaker interviewed about his job; he said that, despite some of the ideas people have about what undertakers do, his work was essentially a way of loving. I think that we can understand his view when we look at this picture of Jesus being entombed by those closest to him.

WB And, of course, this really was the last tomb; there would never be another, because from then onwards everyone would know that the grave was not a final resting-place. It was a station on the way where the body lay awaiting resurrection, a gateway, or springboard into something greater. We may not feel an emotional conviction of this truth, especially when we are grieving over the death of those we love. But it is a truth. God has conquered death and it no longer imprisons us.

WINDOW 15.2; DETAIL

JOSEPH CAST INTO THE PIT

• *Genesis 37: 2-24*

GP In some ways the story of Joseph and his brothers isn't a very suitable parallel to the Passion scene. When we read the story today, Joseph – at least at the beginning – comes across as a prig and given that, and his father's undisguised favouritism, it is not at all surprising that his brothers should have been so envious. A classic case of sibling rivalry! Yet seeing Joseph being cast into the pit by his brothers here reminds us, as do the figures of Judas, Cain and Abel elsewhere in the Chapel, that the most painful fact of human violence is that it is always fratricidal. We are all children of the one God and whoever raises their hand against a fellow human being raises their hand against one who is of their own blood.

WB To be cast into a pit is one of the ulti-mate images of human frailty. Life is not under our control. At any moment events may open up at our feet and there we are, helpless. Christianity is all about believing in salvation from the pit. The pit is real enough: it may be physical pain, financial anxiety, emotional anguish. But we are not helpless. It is not a question of who or what puts us there, but who raises us out. For Joseph it was a temporary rescue, lead-ing to slavery and, only eventually, to glory. But the glory was as real as the pit, and so it will be with us. Indeed, our glory is more real because it will last forever.

WINDOW 15.1; DETAIL

THE RESURRECTION OF CHRIST

GP Nobody would really imagine that Jesus would have stood on top of a stone tomb, carrying a banner and cross as he is here, but that is not important – the artist was not attempting to show what the Resurrection was like, but saying something about what it means. And for me this is very much an image of the triumphant aspect of the Resurrection. Jesus is a serene, joyful figure. He is not looking down in a hostile way at the soldiers who have been guarding his tomb, but his gesture is one of blessing, although it's a blessing that the soldiers are as yet unable to comprehend; it's such a strange, alien event in this history of violence

WB I often grieve that so much is made of the sufferings of our blessed Lord, and so little of what was at the heart of all that suffering, which was our redemption through the Resurrection. So it's wonderful to see that there are several windows in the Chapel which celebrate the poetry of the risen Lord. We all understand sorrow, but so few of us understand joy, and this is a deep, solemn joy. It's not that Jesus is feeling joy, but almost that he *is* joy, and that's why all his actions are those of blessing and blessedness. When the soldiers awoke, they had been invisibly blessed by a presence they didn't even see. What happened burst the bounds of their comprehension, and I understand how they might have felt.

WINDOW 16.2; DETAIL

JONAH CAST UP BY THE WHALE

- *Jonah 1-2*
- *Matthew 12: 40*

GP In the story of Jonah and the whale, the sea monster was regarded as a symbol of the dark depths of the underworld. The story was used by Jesus himself as a parable of death and resurrection. It's an astonishingly forceful image, a huge monster with bulging red eyes, spewing Jonah out of its great gaping black jaws. There's another parallel between the two stories, in that Jonah, like Jesus, was the victim of a violent conspiracy. We are not just seeing Jonah escaping death, but also the defeat of a conspiracy, and now, hopefully, he will be able to go on to fulfil his prophetic mission.

WB The sea monster is an image of death here, and uncontrollable. Many people do see death as something tremendously frightening and awesome, and the way the monster's mouth opens towards us involves us too. It is as if we are all going to be swallowed by the monster, but because of the Resurrection we will emerge into a new life, like Jonah. The difference between Jonah and Jesus was that Jonah thought that he deserved his punishment . To me, the wonderful thing about him is that he used his experience, and emerged into obedience. This links him with Jesus, who was the supremely obedient man.

WINDOW 16.1

THE THREE MARYS AT THE TOMB

- *Matthew 28: 1-8*
- *Mark 16: 1-8*
- *Luke 24: 1-11*
- *John 20: 1-9*

GP Christ has risen from the dead, but as yet no one knows that the Resurrection has happened. In this window we see three women who are amongst those closest to Jesus, his mother, Mary Magdalene, and another of the Marys. They have come to anoint his body with oils, but find him gone. There's no immediate joy for them in this discovery, because they don't imagine that a resurrection has taken place, but think instead that Jesus's body has been stolen. They are sorrowful and bewildered as they look into the empty tomb, and yet also very tender. There is something very loving about that image.

WB To me, this is one of the most beautiful windows in the whole Chapel. I love not only the simplicity of the scene and the solemn grieving beauty of the women, but also the fact that the angel described in the Gospel stories isn't shown so that the women are just looking into nothingness. They have brought their gifts and God hasn't accepted them. They are like the three virtues, Faith, Hope and Charity, all waiting around the tomb, not knowing that the wonderful event has happened, but prepared for it in that they are still standing there. It's that holding on and waiting that in the end leads to the joy of the Resurrection. That prayerful waiting makes them seem very close to the situation of many believers today.

WINDOW 17.2; DETAIL

REUBEN AT THE EMPTY PIT

• *Genesis 37*

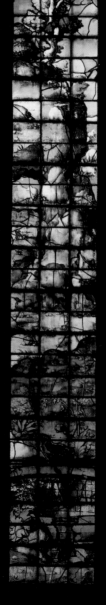

GP After Joseph had been thrown into the pit by his jealous brothers he was sold by them to Midianite slave traders. He was taken to Egypt and imprisoned, but eventually rose to power. This window shows one of his brothers, Reuben, who has come back to the pit to rescue Joseph and finds him gone. Like the women at the tomb, he is appalled, because he doesn't realize that something good will come of this situation, and that he will eventually be reunited with Joseph. What must be particularly painful for Reuben is that he himself had suggested the strategy of putting Joseph in the pit rather than actually killing him, so what he had hoped would turn out for the best has led to disaster.

WB The image of poor Reuben, the one good brother who comes to help Joseph and finds that gaping hole, is a wonderful companion to the picture of the women looking into their gaping tomb. They are all faced with the same mystery, whereby things which seem to be disasters, the very worst things which could happen to us, in the end turn out to be God's triumphs. This theme is, I think, a very hopeful one for us. If we try to do what's right, it will always be a success, because it is the intention which God looks at rather than the outcome. That thought is not much of a consolation for Reuben, though we know differently. He will have years of sorrow, but it's nice to think that the three tender grieving women have only hours to wait.

WINDOW 17.1

45

CHRIST APPEARS TO MARY MAGDALENE (NOLI ME TANGERE)

• *John 20: 14-18*

GP Now we come to the time when the good news breaks, and a new day dawns. We are shown the moment of recognition, when Mary Magdalene sees that the man she thought was the gardener is in fact her Lord and Master. Christ asks her not to touch him (*Noli me tangere*) as he has not yet ascended to his Father, and tells her to go to the disciples to give them the news that he has risen. Her figure is one of the most animated in the whole Chapel. There is a huge tension between attraction and repulsion, repulsion in the sense that she is awestruck and afraid. It's an important image for the contemporary Church, because the discovery of what we might call the apostolate of women is something that belongs very much to our time. Mary Magdalene is in a sense the first Apostle, the first person to take the good news to others. In this sequence of scenes from the Passion we have been discussing, all the male disciples, except for John, disappeared when Jesus was seized in Gethsemane, but the women remained to stand by the cross with John and to care for the body. Now Mary Magdalene, despite the lurid past assigned to her by tradition, has been chosen to be the first witness of the Resurrection. We can see here that her whole being, body and soul, is involved. And Jesus is turning his face in blessing and love on Mary in a movement that sums up what the story of the Passion is about.

WB It's as if Mary can hardly believe what she is seeing, and there is wonder and disbelief fighting in her. It's an experience so overwhelming that she really can't yet feel anything except the impact of the miracle. The wonderful swirl of her garments seems to show her emotions more than her face and hands, which are frozen in astonishment. I presume she didn't recognize him because her eyes were so swollen with tears. And what I find wonderful in this story is that when she asks the gardener, through her blurred eyes, where the body of Jesus is, he says to her, 'Mary' so that she is able to recognize him, and say, 'Rabbuni!', that is 'My Lord and Master'. And I find this idea that God knows our names, and calls us by them very moving. You can see the marks of the nails very clearly on his wounded hands, as he calls her into his risen world, where she can see who he is. What is also emphasized here is that you have to have knelt before Jesus, like Mary Magdalene, and longed for him, and prayed, and opened yourself to hear what he says before you can be an apostle. You can't just do it from reading books, or by external service to God. There has to be an encounter or people will not believe what you tell them. Prayer is letting Jesus look at you and call you by your name, and this is what the Resurrection has given us.

WINDOW 17.4; DETAIL

SUGGESTIONS FOR FURTHER READING

Brown, Raymond, *The Death of the Messiah*. London: G. Chapman, 1994.

Harrison, Kenneth, *The Windows of King's College Chapel, Cambridge*. Cambridge: Cambridge University Press, 1952.

Henry, Avril (ed.), *The Mirour of Mans Saluatione: A Middle English Translation of Speculum Humanae Salvationis*. London: Scolar Press, 1986.

Henry, Avril (cd.), *Biblia Pauperum. A Facsimile Edition*. London: Scolar Press, 1987.

Hilary Wayment, *The Windows of King's College Chapel, Cambridge; A Description and Commentary*. London: Oxford University Press for the British Academy, 1972.

Wayment, Hilary, *King's College Chapel, Cambridge. The Great Windows: Introduction and Guide*. Cambridge: King's College, 1992.